LIFE CYCLE OF A

SUNFLOWER

By Kirsty Holmes

LIFE CYCLES

Words that look like **this** can be found in the glossary on page 24.

BookLife
PUBLISHING

©2021
BookLife Publishing Ltd.
King's Lynn
Norfolk PE30 4LS

ISBN: 978-1-83927-473-2

Written by:
Kirsty Holmes

Edited by:
Shalini Vallepur

Designed by:
Brandon Mattless

A catalogue record for this book is available from the British Library.

PHOTO CREDITS

All images are courtesy of shutterstock.com, unless otherwise specified. With thanks to Getty Images, Thinkstock Photo and iStockphoto. Front Cover & 1 – By ifong, g215. 2&3 – Pablesku. 4&5 – Ami Parikh, Ashwin, StockImageFactory.com, Shyamalamuralinath. 6&7 – Ian 2010, Pakhnyushchy. 8&9 – A_M_Radul, kzww. 10&11 – amenic181, Bogdan Wankowicz. 12&13 – Savchenko Ruslan0212, Somchai Siriwanarangson, Swetlana Wall. 14&15 – Dr Ajay Kumar Singh. 16&17 – DRWelch, kojihirano. 18&19 – AlenKadr, Melinda Fawver, NataliaNM, Katharina Scharle. 20&21 – Daniil Petrov, Gamzova Olga, monticello, MSPhotographic, SaKaLovo. 22&23 – Aliexxandar, Darkdiamond67, Emilio100, Emily Li, Olivkairishka, Stephanie Frey.

WHAT IS A LIFE CYCLE?

All living things have a life cycle. They are all born, they all grow bigger, and their bodies change.

Baby

Child

Toddler

When they are fully grown, they have **offspring** of their own. In the end, all living things die. This is the life cycle.

Teenager

Elderly Person

Adult

SUNNY SUNFLOWERS

Sunflowers are plants. They have long, hairy stems, **broad** leaves and big, yellow flowers. Sunflowers can grow very tall.

Flower

Seeds

Leaf

Stem

These sunflowers are growing in a field on a farm.

Sunflowers can be grown in the garden – they are beautiful and fun to grow. Sunflowers are also an important **crop**.

SUPER SEEDS

Sunflower seeds grow in the centre of the flower. The seeds are small and shaped like teardrops. They are either black and white or black.

The seeds need the right amounts of soil, light, water and warmth to grow. When all of these things are just right, the seed will split open and the plant will begin to grow.

The seed will put out a small shoot, called a radicle.

Seed

Radicle

ROOTS AND SHOOTS

The roots get longer and deeper as the plant grows.

The radicle will grow downwards into the ground. The plant will put out more roots. Roots take in water and **nutrients** from the soil to feed the plant.

The plant's tiny stem, called a shoot, will push upwards through the soil towards sunlight. The shoot will have two green leaves at first.

Leaves

Shoot

LOVELY LEAVES

The sunflower will grow more and more leaves as the stem grows longer. The leaves are broad and dark green.

Some of the bigger leaves may be heart-shaped. Leaves take in **energy** from the Sun, which the plant can use to make food.

Sunflowers usually lean towards the Sun.

SMASHING SUNFLOWERS!

At the top of the stem, a round green **bud** will form. At first, it will look like leaves, but gradually, as the plant grows...

Bud

Flower

... it will open its petals out wide and become a beautiful flower! The flower is large and bright yellow. The seeds are in the centre of the flower.

Petal

The seeds are getting ready to grow as new sunflowers.

Seeds

LIFE AS A SUNFLOWER

Have you ever
grown a sunflower?

Many people grow sunflowers in their gardens.
Some types grow very tall and have enormous flowers.
You can have a competition to see who can grow the
tallest sunflower!

The sunflower will be visited by bees, butterflies, moths and beetles who like to drink its **nectar** for food. The bugs will carry **pollen** from flower to flower.

This is how the flower makes its seeds ready to grow again. It is called pollination.

Bee

Flower

Pollen

FUN FACTS ABOUT SUNFLOWERS

- Sunflowers were first grown in North America.

- Sunflowers need six to eight hours of sunshine per day.

- Sunflowers have been used for medicine, food, **oil** and colours.

- Sunflowers can grow to over three metres tall.

- Not all sunflowers are yellow. There are sunflowers that are stripy, purple or even multi-coloured!

THE END OF LIFE AS A SUNFLOWER

Sunflower Seed Oil

A Super Healthy Snack

A Tasty Topping

Sunflower Seed Butter

Sunflowers are also grown on farms. Sunflower seeds can be eaten, or turned into food and oil. Some seeds are planted so the life cycle continues.

In the autumn, when the seeds are ready, the sunflower will die. The flower will dry up and the seeds fall to the floor.

They will sprout through the soil in the spring, ready to start the life cycle again.

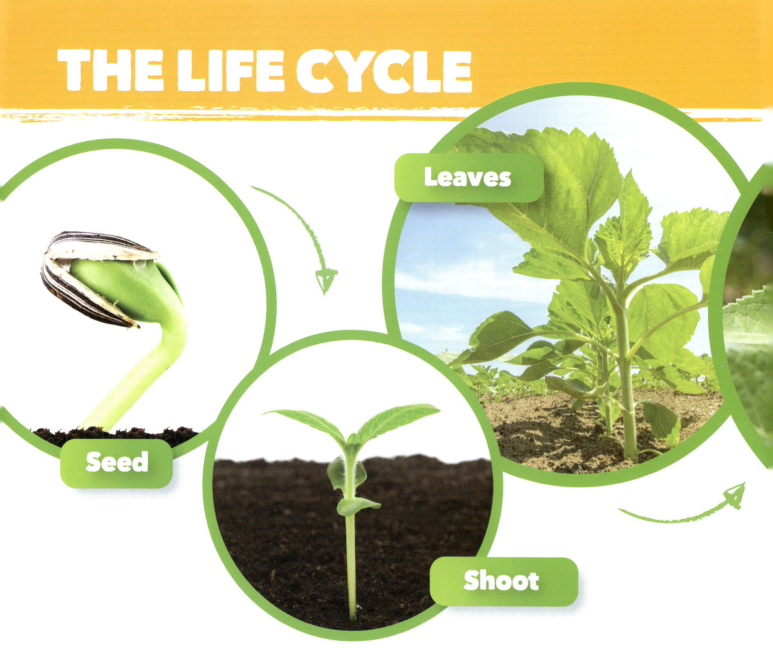

Leaves

Seed

Shoot

A sunflower's life cycle has different stages. Each stage looks very different from the last.

Flower

Bud

New Seeds

In the end, the sunflower dies, and the life cycle is complete.

The seed puts out roots and a shoot. Leaves grow, and the bud blossoms into a bright flower. The flower is pollinated, and the new seeds are ready to fall and start growing.

GLOSSARY

broad wide

bud a small growth on a plant that grows into a leaf, flower or shoot

crop a plant grown on a farm to be used for something

energy a type of power, such as light or heat, that can be used to do something

nectar a sweet liquid made by plants

nutrients natural things that plants and animals need to grow and stay healthy

offspring the babies of an animal or plant

oil a greasy liquid that can be used in cooking

pollen powder that is made by the flowers on a plant

INDEX